A Benjamin Blog
and His Inquisitive Dog
Guide

India

Anita Ganeri

Heinemann
LIBRARY
Chicago, Illinois

Edited by Dan Nunn, Helen Cox Cannons,
and Gina Kammer
Designed by Jo Hinton-Malivoire
Picture research by Ruth Blair and Hannah Taylor
Production by Helen McCreath
Originated by Capstone Global Library Ltd
Printed and bound in Dubai by Oriental Press

18 17 16 15 14
10 9 8 7 6 5 4 3 2 1

Library of Congress
Cataloging-in-Publication Data
Cataloging-in-publication information is on file with
the Library of Congress.
ISBN 978-1-4109-6662-9 (hardcover)
ISBN 978-1-4109-6671-1 (paperback)
ISBN 978-1-4109-6689-6 (eBook PDF)

Acknowledgments
We would like to thank the following for permission
to reproduce photographs:

Alamy: brianindia, 17, Paul Prescott, 15, Stephen
Ford, 14, Stuart Forster, 24, szefei wong, 12, Thomas
Cockrem, 22, travelib history, 7, Universal Images
Group Ltd., 11; Corbis: ZUMA Press/Prasanta Biswas,
27; Getty Images: Amar Grover, 18, Ben Edwards,
13, Danita Delimont, 10, DreamPictures, 23, Joao
Figueiredo, 6, Kurt Werby, 4, Martin Child, 16, Martin
Harvey, 8, Subir Basak, 19; Shutterstock: Globe
Turner, 28, Mazzzur, cover, Rajesh Narayanan, 25,
saiko3p, 26, 29; Superstock: Steve Vidler, 20, Stock
Connection, 9, 21

Every effort has been made to contact copyright
holders of material reproduced in this book. Any
omissions will be rectified in subsequent printings if
notice is given to the publisher.

007015ORISF14

Some words are shown in bold, **like this**. You can find
out what they mean by looking in the glossary.

Contents

Welcome to India!

Hello! My name is Benjamin Blog and this is Barko Polo, my **inquisitive** dog. (He is named after ancient ace explorer, **Marco Polo**.) We have just gotten back from our latest adventure—exploring India. We put this book together from some of the blog posts we wrote on the way.

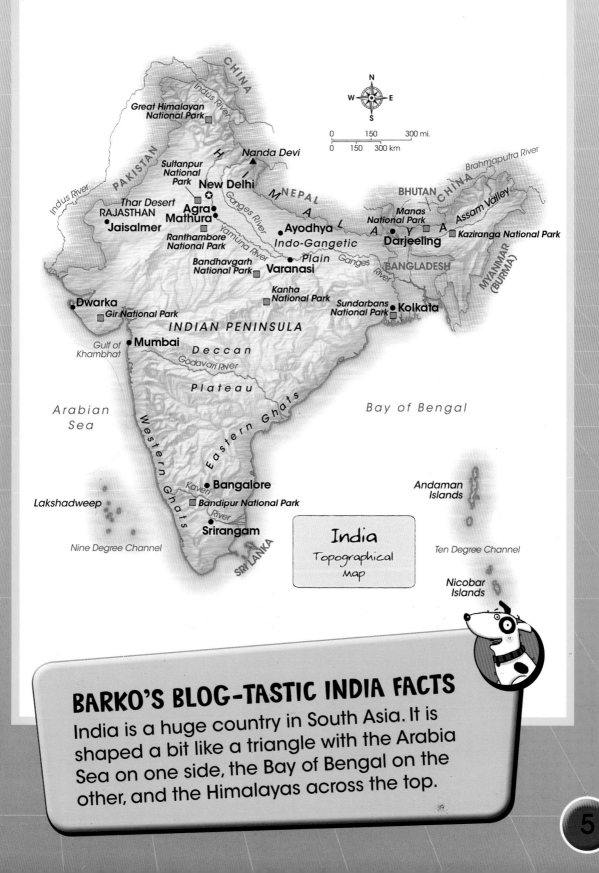

Great Himalayan
National Park

CHINA

Indus River

Nanda Devi

Sultanpur
National
Park

New Delhi

Thar Desert
RAJASTHAN
Jaisalmer

Agra
Mathura

Ranthambore
National Park

Ayodhya

Indo-Gangetic

Plain

Bandhavgarh
National Park

Varanasi

Ganges

Kanha
National Park

Sundarbans
National Park

Kolkata

Dwarka

Gir National Park

INDIAN PENINSULA

Gulf of
Khambhat

Mumbai

Deccan

Godavari River

Plateau

Arabian
Sea

Western Ghats

Eastern Ghats

Bay of Bengal

Bangalore

Kaveri

Bandipur National Park

River

Srirangam

Lakshadweep

Nine Degree Channel

PAKISTAN

Indus River

NEPAL

H I M A L A Y A

BHUTAN

CHINA

Brahmaputra River

Manas
National Park

Assam Valley

Kaziranga National Park

Darjeeling

BANGLADESH

MYANMAR
(BURMA)

Ganges
River

Ganges River

Yamuna River

SRI LANKA

Andaman
Islands

Ten Degree Channel

Nicobar
Islands

India
Topographical
Map

N
W E
S

0   150   300 mi.
0   150   300 km

BARKO'S BLOG-TASTIC INDIA FACTS

India is a huge country in South Asia. It is
shaped a bit like a triangle with the Arabia
Sea on one side, the Bay of Bengal on the
other, and the Himalayas across the top.

Historic Places

Posted by: Ben Blog | December 4 at 10:00 a.m.

We started our tour at Fatehpur Sikri, the ancient capital city built by the **Mughal emperor** Akbar. He ruled India about 450 years ago. Nobody lives here now, but you can wander around the beautiful palaces and have your picture taken next to the grave of Akbar's favorite elephant.

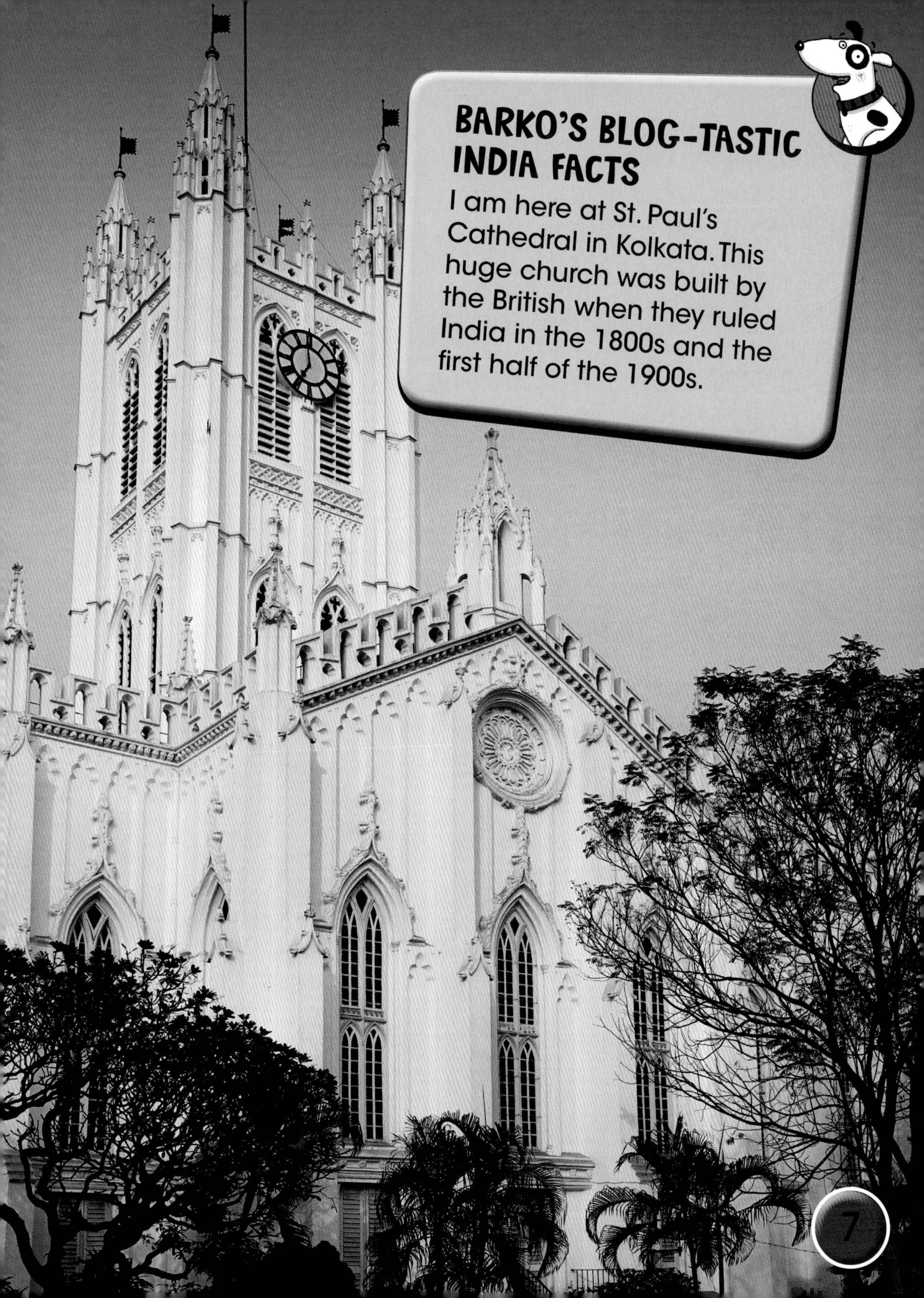

BARKO'S BLOG-TASTIC INDIA FACTS

I am here at St. Paul's Cathedral in Kolkata. This huge church was built by the British when they ruled India in the 1800s and the first half of the 1900s.

Rivers, Mountains, and Deserts

Posted by: Ben Blog | December 18 at 2:10 p.m.

From Fatehpur Sikri, we caught the train to Varanasi on the banks of the Ganges River. The river flows from the Himalayas, across India, and into the Bay of Bengal. For **Hindus**, it is a holy river. They believe that bathing in the water will wash away any bad things they have done.

BARKO'S BLOG-TASTIC INDIA FACTS

This is Nanda Devi, the second-highest mountain in India. The highest mountain is Kanchenjunga. Nanda Devi is 25,643 feet (7,816 meters) tall and part of the awesome Himalayas, the world's highest peaks.

Our next stop was the dusty Thar Desert, where we arrived just in time for the camel festival. It lasts for five days, and people come from all over the desert to buy and sell their camels. There is even a "best-dressed camel" contest. Here is a photo I took of this year's winner.

BARKO'S BLOG-TASTIC INDIA FACTS

In summer, it pours with rain in India. This is called the **monsoon**. Farmers rely on the rain to water their fields, but it can also cause terrible floods.

Crowded Cities

Posted by: Ben Blog | March 30 at 4:36 p.m.

This morning we arrived in New Delhi, India's capital city. What a busy, bustling place. We hitched a ride on a **rickshaw** to the Red Fort in the old part of the city. Like Fatehpur Sikri, the Red Fort was built by the **Mughals**, and it gets its name from its massive red **sandstone** walls.

BARKO'S BLOG-TASTIC INDIA FACTS

Many poor Indian people move to cities in search of work and a better life. Some live in overcrowded parts of the city, called **slums**. Some sleep, wash, and cook on the street.

Namaste!

Namaste means "hello" in Hindi. When you say *namaste*, you put your hands together and bow your head. Hindi is the most commonly spoken language in India, especially here in the north. But there are 21 other main languages and many local **dialects** to learn.

BARKO'S BLOG-TASTIC INDIA FACTS

Indian children often live with their parents, aunts, uncles, cousins, and grandparents. The woman on the left is wearing a **sari**, which are usually made from long pieces of cotton or silk.

In the big cities, many people live in large blocks of apartments. But, a short bus ride out of the city, and we are in the countryside. Most Indian people live in small villages and work by farming the land. They live in small, simple houses with their animals outside.

BARKO'S BLOG-TASTIC INDIA FACTS

In India, children start school when they are 6 years old. These children are on their way to their modern, city school. In villages, lessons are sometimes held outside with children sitting on the ground.

We have traveled south to Tamil Nadu. It is famous for its temples, such as this one at Srirangam. Most Indians are **Hindus**, who follow the religion of **Hinduism**. A temple is a place where they worship. This stunning tower is the gateway to the temple and is covered in carvings of the Hindu gods and goddesses.

BARKO'S BLOG-TASTIC INDIA FACTS

I am celebrating Diwali, the Hindu festival of lights. People light small lamps to guide the god Lord Rama home. Later, there is a spectacular fireworks display.

Feeling Hungry?

Posted by: Ben Blog | November 3 at 6:10 p.m.

All this traveling makes me and Barko hungry, so we stopped for an Indian meal. Most Hindus are vegetarians and do not eat meat. They like to eat spicy vegetables with rice or flatbreads. Here in the south, crispy rice pancakes, called dosas, are very popular. Yummy!

BARKO'S BLOG-TASTIC INDIA FACTS

Indian candy is made from milk, coconut, nuts, sugar, and cream cheese. People make it at home or buy it from candy shops. You give boxes of candy as gifts on special occasions, such as weddings and festivals.

Fun and Games

Posted by: Ben Blog | December 11 at 3:32 p.m.

Next, we flew east to the city of Kolkata to watch a cricket match. Indians are crazy about cricket and play in the street, on the beach, or in the park—wherever they can find space. Members of the Indian cricket team are national heroes. When they are playing, the city comes to a stop.

BARKO'S BLOG-TASTIC INDIA FACTS

Every day, millions of Indians go to the movies to see the latest films. The films are blockbusters, packed with songs, dancing, and action. They are usually at least three hours long. I hope that this one is not sold out!

From TVs to Tea Leaves

Posted by: Ben Blog | December 28 at 8:23 a.m.

My laptop is on the fritz, and I needed to get it fixed. So, we headed to Bangalore, India's center for IT (information technology). Thousands of people work with computers here. Factories in India also make TVs, washing machines, and cars. This has made some Indians very rich but millions of people are still desperately poor.

Fancy a cup of tea? India grows hundreds of thousands of tons of tea and sells it to other countries. Here, in Darjeeling, tea is grown on huge **plantations**. Workers pick the leaves by hand.

And Finally ...

Posted by: Ben Blog | January 3 at 10:17 a.m.

Our trip is nearly over, and we have saved the best for last. We are here in Agra to see the Taj Mahal. It is one of the world's most famous buildings, so I took loads of pictures. It was built in the 1600s by **Mughal emperor** Shah Jahan in memory of his dead wife. What a sight!

BARKO'S BLOG-TASTIC INDIA FACTS

This amazing **mangrove** swamp grows around the Bay of Bengal. It is called the Sundarbans, and it is home to the very rare Bengal tiger. What was that noise?

India Fact File

Area: 1,269,500 square miles
(3,288,000 square kilometers)

Population: 1,220,800,000 (2013)

Capital city: New Delhi

Other main cities: Mumbai; Kolkata

Languages: Hindi and 21 other official languages

Main religions: **Hinduism**; Islam;
Christianity; Sikhism

Highest mountain: Kanchenjunga
(28,209 feet/8,598 meters)

Longest river: Brahmaputra
(1,764 miles/2,840 kilometers)

Currency: Indian rupee

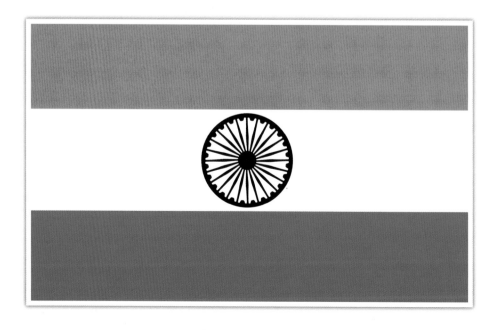

India Quiz

Find out how much you know about India with our quick quiz.

1. What is a **sari**?
a) an Indian candy
b) an Indian piece of clothing
c) an Indian musical instrument

2. What does *namaste* mean?
a) hello
b) good-bye
c) how are you?

3. Where do **Hindus** worship?
a) in a mosque
b) in a church
c) in a temple

4. Which is the most popular sport in India?
a) football
b) kite-flying
c) cricket

5. What is this?

Answers
1. b
2. a
3. c
4. c
5. Taj Mahal

Glossary

dialect a language spoken in a small area or by a small number of people

emperor a ruler

Hindu a person who follows the Hinduism religion

Hinduism an Indian religion, followed by Hindus

inquisitive being interested in learning about the world

mangrove a tree that grows along some tropical coasts

Marco Polo an explorer who lived from about 1254 to 1324; he traveled from Italy to China

monsoon a wind that brings heavy rain

Mughal people who ruled India from the 1500s to the 1800s

plantation a large farm where crops, such as tea and bananas, are grown

rickshaw a small vehicle for carrying passengers, often pulled by a man on a bicycle

sandstone a soft, reddish rock

sari a long piece of cloth that is wrapped around a woman's body

slum an overcrowded part of a city where poor people live

Find Out More

Books

Brownlie Bojang, Ali. *India.*
(Countries Around the World).
Chicago: Heinemann Library, 2012

Ejaz, Khadija. *We Visit India*
(Your Land and My Land).
Hockessin, Del.: Mitchell Lane Publishers, 2013

Powell, Jillian. *India* (My Country).
Mankato, Minn.: Gareth Stevens Pub., 2007

Websites

kids.nationalgeographic.com/kids/places
The National Geographic website has lots of information, photos, and maps of countries around the world.

www.worldatlas.com
Packed with information about various countries, this website includes flags, time zones, facts, maps, and timelines.

Index